Pump it up Magazine

TABLE OF CONTENTS

⚡ ANGELA EASLEY
The Voice of The Bayou
Sultry, Spicy and Full of Soul!

⚡ EDITORIAL 6
Page 5

⚡ SUMMER IN CALI
- The Ultimate California Road Trip
- Books To Read if You're California Dreamin'
- Summer Fairs and Festivals

⚡ TOP TIPS 11
How to book a gig yourself

⚡ WELLNESS
- How to Deal With Toxic People

⚡ FASHION BEAUTY 26
- Look expensive on a budget

⚡ MOVIES 30
Summer Blockbusters

⚡ FITNESS
Fun Ways to exercise this summer

⚡ HUMANITARIAN AWARENESS
How can you select the best charity to support!

MAGAZINE

PUMP IT UP MAGAZINE
LINKS

WEBSITE
www.pumpitupmagazine.com

FACEBOOK
www.facebook.com/pumpitupmagazine

TWITTER
www.twitter.com/pumpitupmag

SOUNDCLOUD
www.soundcloud.com/pumpitupmagazine

INSTAGRAM
pumpitupmagazine

PINTEREST
www.pinterest.com/pumpitupmagazine

PUMP IT UP MAGAZINE
30721 Russell Ranch Road
Suite 140
Westlake Village,
California 91362
United States
www.pumpitupmagazine.com
info@pumpitupmagazine.com
Tel : (001) (877)841 – 7414 (toll free number)

EDITORIAL

Happy summer everyone

The staff here at Pump It Up Magazine hopes everyone is enjoying a safe and fu summer.
The weather here at our headquarters is "hot",
I mean it's hot here in Southern California.
Speaking of heat, wait until you hear this fabulous artist on the cover this month Angela Easley is the embodiment of pure, soul, funk, blues. This talented artist, writer performer and musician has broken down barriers having debuted at # on the Billboard Blues chart and more!
Don't forget to check out her interview in this edition and most of all listen to her single called " Rise".
In our top tips section we have a great article on how to book yourself, especially you haven't landed an agent yet.
What do you think will be the end game with all the changes going on in the wor Are you optimistic that things will get better or worse before it gets better.
I'd like to think that on one side there is optimism and peace and on another pessimism and fear.
Music touches so many emotions that hopefully will allow us to cope with chanç

I hope everyone that reads the magazine has tuned in to KPIU-DB which is Pump I Magazine Radio, with two great shows, The Bernie C show and Grandmixer GM: covering smooth jazz, R&B/Soul and Hip Hop!
Play it proud y'all !

Also check out our section on Summer in Cali..places to go, things to see, road tri good books, concerts and festivals.

In our fashion section you can read about how to look expensive on a budget. self-care challenge. This is good information regarding some of the best care for our health.
Finally we have mental health awareness . How to deal with a toxic person.
I'm sure none of our readers has ever had to deal with that.(wink wink)
That's all for now
Have a great rest of July!
Be well Be Safe!

Anissa Sutton

CONTRIBUTORS

EDITOR IN CHIEF
Anissa Sutton

MUSIC
Michael B. Sutton
Andrew Eug

MARKETING
Grace Rose

PARTNERS

Editions L.A.
www.editions-la.com

The Sound Of L.A.
www.thesoundofla.com

Info Music
www.infomusic.fr

Delit Face
www.DelitFace.com

L.A. Unlimited
www.launlimitedinc.com

**Angela Easley
Photos by Bryan Collins
Angela Easley
is sponsored by**

Angela Easley is a powerful and dynamic vocalist, multi-instrumentalist, prolific songwriter, and radio show host on Radio Free Nashville "103.7 FM and 107.1 FM".
She became the youngest member and lead singer in the band "Bayou Lagniappe" at the age of fifteen. With Bayou Lagniappe, Angela played in many clubs and on festivals across the Nashville region and opened for many artists, including George Jones.

Currently, Angela Easley is a resident of Nashville and occasionally performs with her "Angela Easley Band". The band has achieved wide recognition on the Nashville music scene and has formerly performed on the famous Nashville tourist strip dubbed "Broadway". Angela has also shared a stage at the 3rd and Lindsley with The Wooten Brothers, represented New Orleans alongside NFL Saints player Kyle Turley at Benchmark and has featured at other nightspots, including; The Full Moon Saloon, The Fiddle and Steel Guitar Bar, Paradise Park, and more.
Her latest EP: Rise, is the most recent display of her talent and holds a special meaning to her and many of her fans. She plans on touring and collaborating with other artists in Nashville and all over the US as she embarks on her next studio album.

Blues and Soul music is the foundation for good music of all kinds. The great Willie Dixion said, "Blues is the roots that bare the fruits". A perfect example of an artist that has moved the styles of blues and soul music is the amazing Angela Easley.

Behind a vast discography with tracks considered sultry, spicy, and full of soul, Easley has picked much of her inspiration from great acts such as; Reba, The Judds, Heart, Aretha Franklin, Janis Joplin, Led Zeppelin, and James Brown, among others. Her music borrows heavily from her Mississippi heritage but is also linked to the themes, lyrics, and melodies of the Nashville music hall.

Nashville has contributed greatly to the outspoken voice of singer/songwriter Angela Easley.

Her latest EP dubbed "Rise" released in February 2022 is one of her latest projects that is creating a buzz on many blues and soul music charts and radio stations.
"Rise" is a six-track EP featuring two Grammy-winning artists, including "The McCrary Sisters".

Since its release, the EP has become a chart-regular scooping #1 spot on; Blues Album Billboard charts, Blues Album Soundscan, Single Siriusxm Bluesville Rack of Blues, Album for TN all genres roots music report charts, Single on contemporary Blues Roots music report charts, & Single for TN for all genres roots music report charts. Rise has also debuted as #9 on Digital Radio Tracker and #24 on the Top 25 Blues Albums in Italy.

For the year 2022, the EP could be one of the most decorated blues and soul projects.

Angela Easley

Taking a deep navigation behind the sounds on the EP "Rise," one can surely notice how dynamic and gifted Angela Easley is. All the tracks on the EP carry a little of everything and speak a volume in regards to Easley's ingenuity.
The songs borrow a speck of flavor from the styles of country, rock, funk, gospel, blues and soul music.
Angela Easley disclosed that her latest EP is an anthem and a message to everybody.

"The only way we rise is if we come together and RISE TOGETHER".

Alongside having some of the greatest features on this EP,

Rise is a call for peace, hope, and healing for a world that desperately needs healing right now. The global theme of the EP is Love.

On the single "Rise," for instance, there is a voice of call to action. When people come together as one, they have power. In the world today where we pre-exist with wars and weapons, one way to tame mankind to live in harmony with one another is to rise up together for each other. Love is lost, and gained, but above everything, it overcomes all.

The gifted Angela Easley chose the path of encouraging all her fans and listeners with an uplifting track list that unites and will touch your soul on a deep level.

Indeed, the EP "Rise" is very assimilating and well thought-out. The artist's mollified vocals gave each track a much-needed transfusion of new blood while she stayed true to the roots.

Her track "Running Out of Time" accompanied a rock-kind of vibe that displayed her versatility as an artist that can blend in the current styles. What is different about Angela Easley from many other blues and soul artists, is her adept songwriting skills and a good ear for music.

All of her songs encompass a melody that may seem relatable to the ear but is often unknown with the lyrics that are manifested.

"I Can Let Go" featuring "The McCrary Sisters" is a classic that can be used for the precedent. There are standards in terms of the production and vocal ability if it comes to renowned acts such as Easley and the McCrary Sisters. However, with so much simplicity, they both delivered a sweet aroma that is not foreign to the ear but in a fashion that was expected from two talented generations. If you are familiar with Angela Easley from her Bayou Lagniappe days, you can surely relate to her agility.

Artists such as Tina Turner, and the whole Motown movement jazz songs, with rock and roll blues, emerged as a different genre to the rock and roll of the 50s.
Currently, Angela Easley has also given rise to the rhythm of soul and blues being seen as a piece of legitimate popular music.

She has become one of the famous Nashville faces and is respected as a performer, Award-winner, radio show host, and outstanding instrumentalist.

www.AngelaEasley.com

Angela Easley

1. GREAT TO HAVE YOU ON PUMP IT UP MAGAZINE! PLEASE TELL US ABOUT YOUR BACKGROUND

Angela Easley

Hi, I am Angela Easley. I grew up in Poplarville, MISSISSIPPI. I have lived in Nashville, TN now. I have lived here 18 years now.

2. HOW DID YOU GET STARTED IN THE MUSIC BUSINESS?

Angela Easley

Being a guest on any podcast can you, the artist
I started singing in Church at 8 years old. I would sing at talent shows n festivals around the area.
At 14, I won a talent show that landed me the opportunity to perform on the stage of The Grand Ole Opry & a two single recording session. That sparked my dream and my love affair with Nashville.
I then became the lead vocalist for the band Bayou Lagniappe out of Slidell,
LA. We did a lot of amazing things including opening for George Jones which I got to perform with on stage
After high school, I started the Angela Easley Band and I have been going strong ever since.

3. TELL US WHAT'S THE STORY BEHIND YOUR NEW EP AND SONG "RISE".

Angela Easley

RISE is anthem and message to all that the only way we RISE is if we come together and RISE TOGETHER.

RISE is a message of peace, hope, and healing for a world that desperately needs it right now.

The overall them of the EP is love. Love lost, love gained, and love overcomes all. It is the story of my
heart to encourage all who listen.

4. WHAT MAKES YOUR PRODUCTIONS UNIQUE? AND HOW WOULD YOU DESCRIBE IT?

Angela Easley

My music is like Gumbo from where I am from. It has a little of everything and it's good for the soul. It has a little flavor of country, blues, rock, soul, funk, and gospel music.

5. WHO ARE YOUR BIGGEST MUSICAL INFLUENCES? AND ANY PARTICULAR ARTIST/BAND YOU WOULD LIKE TO COLLABORATE WITH IN THE FUTURE?

Angela Easley

My influences range from REBA, THE JUDDS, HEART, ARETHA FRANKLIN, JANIS JOPLIN, LED ZEPPELIN, JAMES BROWN & MORE

I WOULD LOVE TO COLLABORATE WITH REBA & HEART.

6. WHICH IS THE BEST MOMENT IN YOUR MUSICAL CAREER THAT YOU'RE MOST PROUD OF?

Angela Easley

I have many but I recently saw a life long dream come true. My album RISE debuted as #1 Blues Album on Billboard Charts & more. I am so grateful!!!

7. IF YOU HAD ONE MESSAGE TO GIVE TO YOUR FANS, WHAT WOULD IT BE?

Angela Easley

Don't Give UP! Keep going!

8. WHAT'S NEXT FOR YOU? ANY UPCOMING PROJECTS OR TOURS?

Angela Easley

Touring, producing other artists in Nashville, songwriting, start recording my next album

Listen to "Rise" on KPIU RADIO
INDIE PLAYLIST EVERYDAY AT 6PM PST
WWW.KPIURADIO.COM

Keep up with Angela Easley's music through her website
HTTPS://ANGELAEASLEY.COM
and on all her social and music media platforms.

Facebook: @angelaeasleymusic
Twitter: @angelaeasley
Instagram: @angela_easley
TikTok: @angelaeasleymusic
YouTube: @angelaeasleymusic
AppleMusic: angela-easley
Spotify: angelaeasley

TOP TIPS

HOW TO BOOK A GIG YOURSELF

1. FIND OUT WHAT'S GOING ON NEAR YOU

Follow local venues and events organisers on social media and sign up to their mailing lists so if they're on the hunt for acts, you'll be first to know. Follow other local bands so if they put a shout out for a support act, you'll be ready to show your interest.

2. TRY AND IDENTIFY SUITABLE VENUES

A lot of venues will offer a varied program of music, but some are more specialised. If there's a venue that particularly suits your genre and style, you'll be in with a good chance of making a compelling case for playing there.

Similarly, it's worth taking note of potential venues' capacities. Naturally, it makes sense to start small and work your way up. If word spreads that your band played a brilliant sold out gig at a small local venue, you may be able to use this as a springboard for playing a bigger one next time..

3. MAKE IT EASY FOR THE PERSON CONSIDERING BOOKING YOUR BAND

When you're getting ready to contact a venue, it's worth bearing in mind that they probably receive a lot of gig applicants every day. If you can show that you've considered what you're sending, made it concise, informative and easy to view, you'll be in with more of a chance than someone who has written too little, too much, or failed to highlight the things that make their band interesting and potentially saleable.

It's a good idea to create a pack or 'EPK' containing press and live shots, your logo, a short bio (written in third person) and links to your social media pages. Don't forget the music. Have a couple of your finest tracks prepared, or better still a high quality live performance video. Chances are, a venue or promoter will prefer to receive these as links, rather than whopping files that might break their inbox. Pick the things that show what you do best, including review snippets and previous performances at comparable venues or with notable acts.

4. FIND OUT WHO THE RIGHT PERSON TO CONTACT IS

Social media has a lot of uses when it comes to gig promotion, but if you approach a venue this way to ask for a gig, chances are you won't be reaching the music programmer. Most venue websites will list their programmer's name and email (although you might have to do some digging).

Call them by their name and send an email that is tailored to them, or, better still, give them a call or arrange to pop in for a chat. As with lots of other things in life, booking gigs is considerably easier if you can form a rapport with the person in charge.

Editions L.A.

DIGITAL CREATIVE AGENCY

We Transform Your Vision Into Creative Results

Editions L.A. is a full-service agency based in Los Angeles. Our company is a collective of amazing people striving to build delightful services
We believe that is all about getting your message across clearly and with a "Wow!" thrown in for good measure.

Our Awesome Services

Branding

We build, style and tone your brand identity from the ground up.
We rebrand established bands, brands or businesses.

Merchandise Store
Website design and E-Commerce
Website updates

Digital Marketing

CD Cover | Banners | Logo design | Flyers | Brochures | Leaflets | Print ads | Magazine covers & artworks
Facebook / twitter / instagram / youtube artworks
| Book cover
Infographics | Icon Design |
| TshirtsProduct Labels | Presentation slides
Corporate graphics
Professional photo editing & enhancing
Redesign existing elements
YouTube Optimization and Monetization
Youtube Video Editing
Lyric Video and Advertising Design.

Publishing

BOOK COVER DESIGN
EBOOK FORMATTING SERVICES
and distribution on major platforms
(Amazon, Barnes & Nobles..)

Tell us about your dream and we will make it true!

Editions L.A.
7210 Jordan Avenue Suite B42, Canoga Park, California 91303, United States
info@edtions-la.com
Website: www.editions-la.com

6. MANAGE YOUR FINANCIAL EXPECTATIONS (BUT NOT TOO MUCH)

Bands should absolutely receive money to perform, so it's a gargantuan red flag if you are actually asked to pay to play somewhere, as can happen - particularly in larger cities. When it comes to money, there are a few different arrangements you might encounter, which have differing levels of risk and reward.

Bookings with guaranteed fees are ideal because you know exactly what you'll be getting. Due to the level of risk this may bring to the venue (who will also have to take into account overheads and staffing costs) these gigs can be hard to come by, especially if you're not an established name just yet.

Therefore, it can be a smart idea to ask for a co-promotion with a ticket split rather than a guarantee. This will show the venue that you're willing to work to promote the event because the amount of tickets sold directly impacts the amount of money you'll earn. In many cases, a co-pro will actually work out better for both parties than a booking with a guarantee, which is likely to be on the conservative side to reduce the venue's risk.

You may be offered the option of hiring the venue. This can be a good route if you are confident about filling the space, but an arrangement like this shifts all risk on to the band, and it's possible to make a loss if you don't sell enough tickets.

7. TAKE THE FIRST STEPS FOR PROMOTING YOUR GIG

It's most impactful to coordinate an announcement date with the venue. Once this has been agreed, create a Facebook event, add the venue and any support acts as co-hosts and be sure to invite your existing followers and friends. Echo this on your other social media pages, and share the event in local 'What's On' groups, or related pages. The venue should list your event on their website, but it's always worth asking if there's anything else they can do to help via their social channels and mailing lists.

Create a poster to distribute online and in the real world. Use a compelling live shot as the main focal point as this will convey better than anything else the type of band you are, and what your performances are like. Try and get your posters in locations where music fans are likely to be - like record shops, guitar shops or other venues and pubs.

8. KEEP THE MOMENTUM GOING

As the gig approaches, ramp-up your promotional activities and try other ideas. Clips showing band rehearsals can drive engagement, as can creative social media videos that show how excited the band is, or that convey positive messages such as fast ticket sales.
If you have a little bit of budget, it may be worth considering paid promotions on social media, especially if you are looking to fill a larger venue than you have previously.

YOUR MUSIC CONSULTANT

"You Believe And So Do We!"

YOUR MUSIC CONSULTANT
"YOU BELIEVE, SO DO WE!"

We Can Help You To Grow Your Business

We are a monthly based service, we put faith in artists who has major potential, believed in them, and who are willing to spend their time and own money to work with us in building a successful music career!

Digital Marketing Services

SOCIAL MEDIA - STREAMING SERVICES - MUSIC DISTRIBUTION - PRESS RELEASE - PRESS DISTRIBUTION - PR

Radio Airplay and TV Commercial

TERRESTRIAL AND DIGITAL RADIO CAMPAIGN AL GENRES EXCEPT HEAVY METAL - CABLE TV AND MAJOR NETWORK COMMERCIAL

Licensing & Booking

CONCERTS, LIVE MUSIC, EVENTS, CLUB NIGHTS - RED CARPETS - FOREIGN LICENSING AND SUB0PUBLISHING

Why Choose Us ?

3 DECADES OF MUSIC BUSINESS EXPERIENCE
Platinum and Gold Records
MOTOWN RECORDS
UNIVERSAL
SONY
CAPITOL RECORDS

WE WORKED WITH:
Kanye West - Jay Z - Stevie Wonder - Michael Jackson - Germaine Jackson - Smokey Robinson - Dionne Warwick - Cheryl Lynn - The Originals -

📞 **1-818-514-0038**
(Ext. 1)
Monday - Friday / 9am to 6pm

FIND US :

www.YourMusicConsultant.com
30721 Russell Ranch Road Suite 140 Westlake Village, USA
Email : info@yourmusicconsultant.com

DIGITAL RADIO TRACKER

Leading global broadcast monitoring source that tracks radio airplay of songs in the US and worldwide on more than 5000+ radio stations.

Register for a FREE DRT Account Now!

DIGITALRADIOTRACKER.COM
INFO@DIGITALRADIOTRACKER.COM

ANEESSA

"Miles Away"

A dreamy smooth jazz song that will call you back to a place of comfort.

WWW.ANEESSA.COM

SUMMER

THE PERFECT VACATION

- *The Ultimate California Road Trip*
- *Books To Read if You're California Dreamin'*
- *Summer Fairs and Festivals*

THE ULTIMATE CALIFORNIA ROAD TRIP

1. CALIFORNIA'S PACIFIC COAST HIGHWAY (HIGHWAY 1)

Start: Dana Point (Orange County)
End: Leggett (Mendocino County)
Distance: 656 miles
Recommended time: At least five days (if you can, take a week or two to explore)

2. THE EASTERN SIERRAS (HIGHWAY 395)

Start: Lone Pine
End: South Lake Tahoe
Distance: 232 miles
Recommended time: Four to five days

3. THE BEST OF NORTHERN CALIFORNIA: HIGHWAY 128

Start: Winters
End: Elk
Distance: 140 miles
Recommended time: Three to four days

4. NORTHERN CALIFORNIA WINE COUNTRY ROAD TRIP IN NAPA AND SONOMA

Start: San Francisco
End: San Francisco
Distance: 161 miles
Recommended time: Two or three days

5. REDDING TO LASSEN VOLCANIC NATIONAL PARK

Start: Redding
End: Lassen Volcanic National Park
Distance: 188 miles
Recommended time: Three to five days

6. GOLD CHAIN HIGHWAY (HIGHWAY 49)

Distance: 295 miles
Start: Oakhurst
End: Vinton
Recommended time: Five or six days

BOOKS TO READ IF YOU CALIFORNIA DREAMIN'

1. WHERE I WAS FROM
by Joan Didion

Native Californian Joan Didion takes a look at her home state in this thoughtful, well-researched book. Both proud of and dissatisfied with her home of California, she explores both the past and present, ranging on topics from robber barons, to water crises, to thoughts on individualism versus the incarceration. Didion's craft shines throughout the text, and her passion for this beautiful, complex and often contradictory place draws us in

2. GOOD VIBRATIONS
by Mike Love and James S. Hirsch

The New York Times bestselling Good Vibrations tells the story of Mike Love's legendary, raucous, and ultimately triumphant five-decade career as the front man of the Beach Boys, the most popular American band in history.

3. THE GIRLS
by Emma Cline

One of the most buzzworthy books of the summer, Emma Cline's novel takes place in 1960s Northern California, following teenage Evie Boyd. Like many young girls, she feels lonely and out-of-place — that is, until she meets the mesmerizing Suzanne, and is drawn into a group of people following a dangerously charismatic man. A taut, psychological read, this is a coming-of-age tale like no other.

4. EAST OF EDEN
by John Steinbeck

In this sprawling epic of the Salinas Valley of California, the Trask and Hamilton families live out their own versions of Biblical stories. The fall of Adam and Eve, the rivalry of Cain and Abel, are reenacted by these unwitting participants as they love, betray and shed blood in the rich farmlands of the valley.

Are you a songwriter or composer struggling to protect your work and releases?
*Well **Bernie Capodici** has done all the work for you in his new book*
"Modern Recording Artist Handbook, How To Guide Simplified"

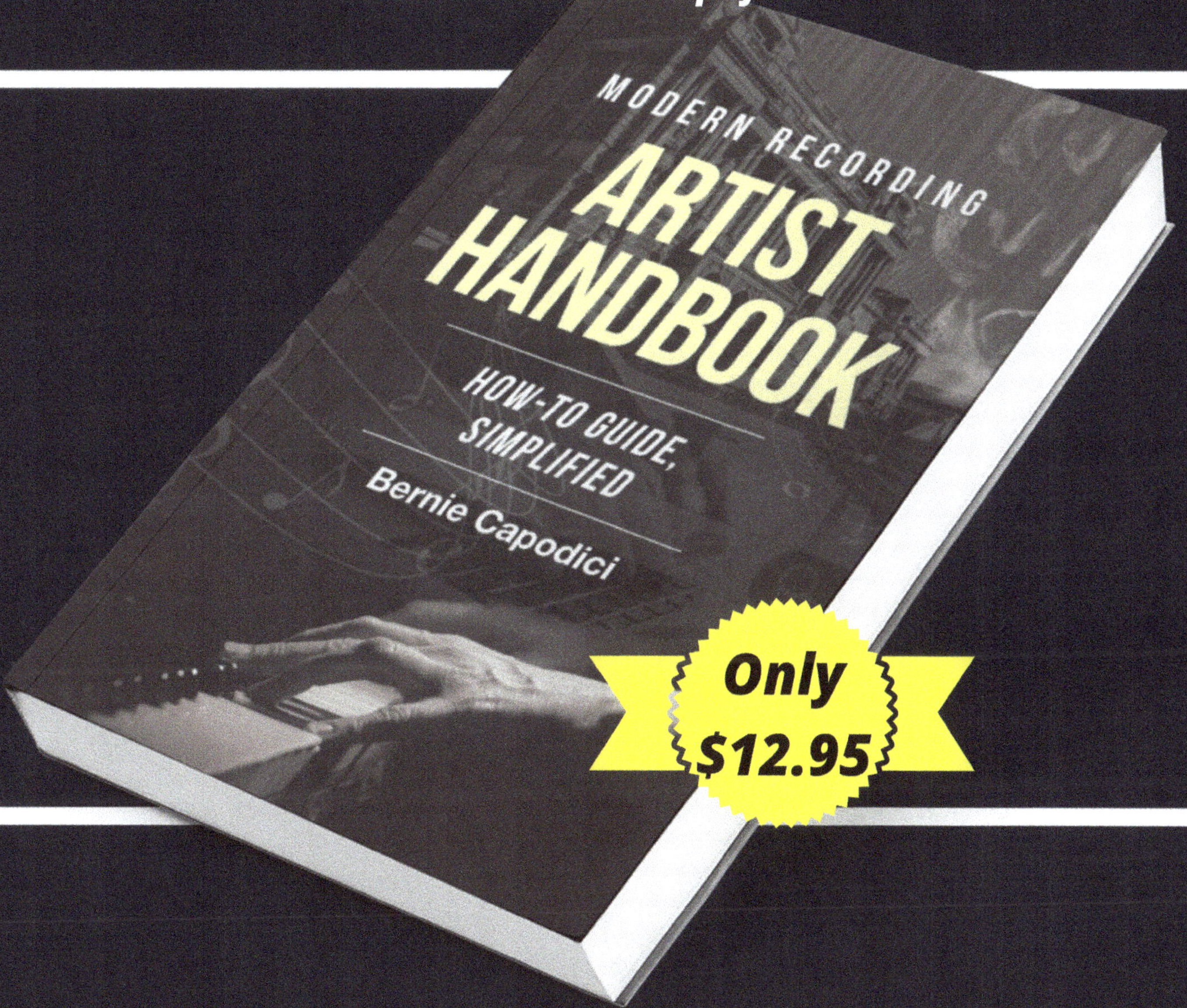

Only $12.95

MUST READ FOR INDEPENDENT ARTISTS

KINDLE $9.99 - HARDCOVER $22.95 - PAPERBACK $12.95

FAIRS AND FESTIVALS

@pumpitupmagazine

SUMMER EVENTS

www.pumpitupmagazine.com

1. VENTURA COUNTY FAIR

This year the Ventura County Fair is themed "Rooted in Tradition" and runs from the end of July to mid-August at the Fairgrounds,
The Fair features live entertainment, contests, lots of exotic fried food, nostalgic and modern games and rides, horseshoes, and everything else you would expect from a county fair.
10 W. Harbor Blvd., Ventura adjacent to the Ventura Pier.

2. MUSIC 4 THE SOUL FEATURING DRAMATICS, DELFONICS, SLY SLICK AND WICKED & MORE
REDONDO BEACH PERFORMING ARTS CENTER

On behalf of GEMs Reaching Educational Milestones presents Music 4 The Soul, featuring The Dramatics with LJ Reynolds, Delfonics, Sly Slick and Wicked along with Seville Ohio Trio plus Yvette Cook hosted by Lamarr Deuce Lubin. Join us for a trip down memory lane as these legends perform their hits, "Whatca See Is Whatca Get," "In the Rain," "LaLa Meaans I love You," "Hey You" and more. A portion of the proceeds raised will Benefit GEMs a high school placement program that helps students matriculate to private high schools.
Wed, Jul 20, 2022
1935 Manhattan Beach Blvd.
Redondo Beach, CA 90278
310-937-6607

3. FOUNTAIN VALLEY BBQ MUSIC FEST
Fountain Valley BBQ Music Fest will be held on
August 19-21, 2022. It will feature live entertainment, children's area, petting zoo,..
Fountain Valley Sports Park
16400 Brookhurst Street
Fountain Valley, CA 92708

L.A. UNLIMITED

APPAREL REPRESENTATION
WITHOUT LIMITS...

- Corporate Brand Representation
- Brand Identity & Management
- Brand Consulting
- Trade Show Preparation & Participation
- Trunk Shows
- Private Label Sales
- Production Sourcing

L.A. Unlimited & Associates
30765 Pacific Coast Hwy STE 443Malibu, CA 90265

310.882.6432
sales@launlimitedinc.com

FASHION & BEAUTY

HOW TO LOOK EXPENSIVE ON A BUDGET

1. WEAR BLACK

Black is a neutral, it goes with everything. Since it is a solid color it coordinates with other colors and patterns. When we think of the color black, we think of Coco Chanel. She made the colors black and white famous in her tailored clothes and fabrics.

2. MONOCHROME IT OUT

One of the easiest ways to add extra spice to an outfit is with tonal or monochrome pieces. Theodora often styles her clients in identical colored tops and skirts while changing the textures to add a bit of dimension. Monochrome outfits are not only incredibly elongating, but they look effortless, put together, and very expensive.

3. ADD A BLAZER

Amanda Greyson, style director at Free People, believes blazers are the surefire way at elevating even the simplest of outfits. "Try adding a blazer to a simple hoodie and denim look, finishing with a baseball hat and high-top trainers," she suggests. "This will instantly make your look feel more luxe for all those weekend errands. Or, for date night, add an oversized blazer to a silk black dress and easy bootie."

4. WEAR PIECES THAT FIT WELL

Always make sure your clothes fit well. If you have an hourglass figure, wear pieces that fit showing off your curves. If you have a few pounds in areas you want to conceal, opt for pieces that are slightly loose and flow when you walk. For all figures, avoid wearing clothes that are too loose..

5. SPLURGE ON A STRONG BLACK COAT

Invest in classic, high-quality outerwear in timeless black or camel colorways. It will last you decades. Classic styles never expire and will carry you through every decade—warm.

FASHION & BEAUTY

24 - 34

6. WEAR POINTED FLATS OR HEELS

Women who wear flats or heels that are pointed have a look that screams expensive! Black or nude are popular colors that go with everything. They are considered wardrobe essentials.

6. WEAR LIPCOLOR

Wear makeup that looks natural and wear lipcolor. Wear a lipcolor that has a colored tint, like red, coral or pink. Red is a classic lipcolor. It goes great with black and white. Wear a shade of red that looks good with your skin tone. Make sure your nails are kept trimmed and/or painted.

7. COORDINATE YOUR SHOES & BAG

A key to making your outfits look polished is coordinating your shoes and bag. If you wear black shoes then carry a black bag. Brown shoes look great with a brown bag in the same color tone. You can venture out a bit by wearing black shoes with a nude or a solid color bag, like pink. Leopard flats or heels look great with a black or nude bag.

8. WEAR SUNGLASSES

Wear sunglasses and you'll look cool and collected! Perhaps the images of celebrities wearing beautiful sunglasses have been an influence to us to wear them.
The fancier the sunglasses help make your outfit look expensive. black sunglasses, aviator sunglasses, cat-eye sunglasses, leopard sunglasses

9. WEAR STATEMENT JEWELRY

Wear jewelry that makes a statement. Fancy jewelry adds a polished look to any outfit. When your outfit is basic, like black pants and white top, add a statement necklace, earrings bracelet and you outfit instantly looks "glam"!

EXERCISE IN SUMMER THAT WON'T FEEL LIKE A CHORE!

1. ROLLERSKATING
Roller skating is an aerobic workout that increases coordination and balance. This retro pastime doesn't just look cool, it also leaves your body feeling great.

2. BIKE RIDE
Whether you're one of our crazy intense cyclers in our PK fam, or just down for a slower family ride along the beach- biking is an excellent workout, and so much fun!

3. FAVORITE CHILDHOOD GAME
Nothing like taking yourself back to days when the living was easy! There is a part of me that will never give up on capture the flag no matter how old. I just wish someone would ask me to play (hint, hint).

4. DANCING (ZUMBA, SWING..)
Ready to try something new? Join a dance class! When you leave I promise you'll be weating up a storm, and the best part is dancing is so fun!

5. HAVE A WALKING MEETING
Do you often plan meetings with your coworkers to just sit around and talk? Take that meeting outside and talk as you go for a group walk!

6. HIKING
There is nothing like a good hike, the burn in your legs, the fresh air, the views. Hiking will never feel like a chore to me, more of a release from everyday life!

7. ACTIVE VIDEO GAMES
Active video games are truly the best! They're so fun, and you can really work up a sweat quick if you do it right!

HAVE FUN!

WELLNESS   27 - 34

SELF CARE CHALLENGE

WELLNESS TIPS

Stay offline for the whole day	Stay away from toxic people	Learn to enjoy solitude
Read a self-help book	Preserve positive thoughts	Meditate or do yoga
Clean your room	Declutter your living space	Write a daily journal
Try something new	Eat more vegetables	Examine your daily habit
Change up your routine	Turn off notifications	Consume less dairy
Lay off the caffeine	Practice Gratitude	Go for a walk in the nature

HOW TO DEAL WITH TOXIC PEOPLE

1. RECOGNIZE WHAT MAKES YOU AN EASY PREY
Is it often your fear of rocking the boat or the need to please them that keeps you tongue-tied when your "friend" takes it out on you. Use rational thinking to process the interactions you have had with the friend that made you unhappy. Focus on why you felt what you did, not what you felt, and try to decipher if you can get a pattern.

2. MOVE ON WITHOUT THEM
If you know a friend who always destructively dictates the emotional atmosphere, be sure of this – they are toxic. If you are suffering because of a person's attitude, and your patience, advice, compassion, and attentiveness do not seem to help them, and they don't seem to care a bit, ask yourself, "Do I really need this human in my life?" When you remove toxic people from your life, it becomes way easier to breathe.

3. PUT YOUR FOOT DOWN
Your dignity may be ravaged, attacked, and mocked, but it can never be taken away from you unless you surrender it willingly. It is all about finding the self-love to defend your boundaries. Make it clear that you won't allow anyone to insult or belittle you. You can effectively end conversations that are putting you down with plain abruptness or sickening sweetness. The message should be clear – you will entertain no games.

4. STOP ACCEPTING THEIR TOXIC BEHAVIOR
Toxic people often use their moody and loud behavior to get preferential treatment. You may find it easier to quiet them down by giving in to their demands than listen to their nagging. Don't be fooled into doing this.
Short-term comfort will equal long-term headache for you in a situation like this. Toxic people won't change if they get rewarded for not changing. Constant negativity and drama are never worth putting up with.

5. SPEAK UP
Stand up for yourself. Some people can do anything for their personal gain at the expense of others – take your money and property, pass guilt, cut in line, bully and belittle others, etc. Do not accept this kind of behavior. These people know what they are doing is wrong. They will back down considerably quickly when confronted. In most social settings, people tend to be quiet until one person speaks up. So, speak up!

6. PRACTICE PRACTICAL COMPASSION
You aren't really helping someone by accepting everything they do just because they have issues. There are a lot of people who go through extreme hardships, but they are not toxic to others around them. We can only be genuinely compassionate when we set respectful boundaries. Making too many allowances and pardons is not healthy for anyone in the long-term. Always remember, even people with clinical/mental illnesses or legitimate problems can comprehend that you may have your own needs as well, which means you need to politely excuse yourself when you feel things are getting out of hand. You deserve this 'me' time. You deserve to live peacefully, free from toxic behavior and external pressure, with no boundaries to uphold, problems to solve, or people to please.

WEST END ORGANIX

Ageless Beauty, Organic Health

Look and feel younger and healthier with our natural remedies products!

www.WestEndOrganix.com

Discount: 10% off of your order - Code *WEO2021*

SUMMER BLOCKBUSTERS

1. ELVIS

This biopic about Elvis Presley starring Austin Butler and Tom Hanks comes to us from director Baz "Moulin Rouge" Luhrmann, and will hopefully delve into how the hound dog hater himself (and his mysterious manager Colonel Tom Parker, played by Hanks) stole music from Black people so unabashedly that it's borderline sociopathic. We bet it's real dramatic and you'll find think pieces all over the internet about it.

2. THOR: LOVE AND THUNDER

Usually we'd be like, "Good lord, more Marvel?!" but remember that the Thor movies are now made under the watchful eye of New Zealand treasure Taiki Waititi. We're not saying that means it'll go into conversations alongside Casablanca or anything, but it'll at least be fun and funny. In this one, Natalie Portman returns to, I dunno, also be Thor or something? A villain appears, other Marvel characters appear, the "good" side wins, and probably by the skin of their teeth. Christian Bale's in this one, as are the Guardians of the Galaxy and, of course, Chris Hemsworth (he's Thor).

3. BULLET TRAIN

Brad Pitt and Sandra Bullock come together in a movie about a bunch of assassins on a bullet train who must kill their target on the bullet train, but who learn that maybe the bullet train ride isn't the only thing they and the other bullet train riders have in common. Bullet train.

4. A LOVE SONG

The ever-excellent Dale Dickey (No Exit) and Santa Fe hometown hero Wes Studi play a pair of former high school relationship-havers who wind up widowed and back in each other's lives after so many years. Our guess? This will be sweet and poignant and brilliantly acted.

5. LIGHTYEAR

Chris Evans voices Pixar's Buzz Lightyear in the CGI origin story movie no one asked for. We bet it ends all like, "...and that's why friendship in space matters, Buzz!" Cue Randy Newman song. Cue tears that were emotionally manipulated out of you.

6. JURASSIC WORLD DOMINION

We know what you're thinking, and you're right—it IS sad that Chris Pratt and Bryce Dallas Howard keep doing these lesser Jurassic Park sequels. BUT LIFE FINDS A WAY! Which is to say that Sam Neil is returning as Dr. Alan Grant, the very character who inspired a generation of 10-year-olds to wear kerchiefs and get into science to stop a potential kitchen-based raptor attack

FUN QUIZZES | 31 - 34

MY MUSIC LIST

_____
A SONG THAT MAKES ME HAPPY

_____
A SONG FROM THE 70s

_____
A SONG ABOUT YOUR COUNTRY

_____
A SONG WITH A COLOR

_____
A SONG YOU CAN'T LISTEN ANYMORE

SHARE THIS LIST WITH YOUR FRIENDS

ALBUM CHALLENGE

_____
DEBUT ALBUM

_____
CONCEPT ALBUM

_____
80'S ALBUM

_____
LIVE ALBUM

_____
SOUNDTRACK

_____
FAVORITE ALBUM

This or That

What would you choose?

Get up early or Stay up late

Talk to dogs or Talk to cats

Lose your sense of taste or Lose your sense of smell

Give up on music or Give up on movies

Read minds or Know everything

Travel to the future or Travel to the past

WHAT WOULD YOU PREFER...
RANDOM EDITION

Live in the city or Live in the countryside

Play video games or Play board games

Lose your phone or Lose your wallet

Speak many languages or Speak with animals

Own a private island or Own a private jet

Live without music or Live without TV

Pump it up Magazine / 31 - 34

HOW TO SELECT THE BEST CHARITIES TO SUPPORT

1. AM I PASSIONATE ABOUT THIS CHARITY?

Decide what you're passionate about before choosing a charity. Organizations focused on animals, education, health, homelessness, hunger, religion and civic issues are all popular. And most charities that address those issues need help year-round to meet the needs of their constituents.

You're sure to make a wise charity choice if you go with those that are most meaningful to you and your family.

2. IS THIS CHARITY LEGITIMATE OR THE ONE I THINK IT IS?

Make sure a charity with a local phone number and address is serving those in your community. Also, as news accounts have shown in recent years, lots of charities adopt names very similar to those of nationally known organizations but don't represent those organizations.

First, learn what a public charity is from the IRS. Then, check to see if the charity is licensed in your state.

Next, check the charity's reputation with the Better Business Bureau's Wise Giving Alliance or by searching online for media coverage and social media rankings of the organization. Then, check Charity Navigator, the American Institute of Philanthropy's Charity Watch or GuideStar to see if it's a legitimate charity, and to get ratings and recent news on charities.

If you're considering a religious organization or ministry, go to MinistryWatch and Evangelical Council for Financial Accountability for information on those organizations. Talk to others who've donated to them, too.

All of these sites have multiple resources related to choosing charities well. So spend quality time on them learning about choosing charitable organizations before you make any donations.

3. WHAT ARE MY FINANCIAL POSITION AND PLAN FOR GIVING?

Know whether you're in a financial position to give what you're being asked to give. Avoid acting on emotional appeals to give. Take some time between the appeal and decision to think clearly about your donation.

Don't allow yourself to be pressured into making contributions you can't afford or committing to pledge plans that don't fit your long-term budget. Because charitable donating is a form of investment, determine your level of comfort with investing in charities and only invest as much as you're comfortable giving.

Then, have a plan for giving. "Create a giving budget. Will you give once a year in a big lump sum to 2 or 3 charities? Or would you rather set up a small monthly donation to each," suggests Miniutti.

Think about how your giving fits into your overall financial plan and, depending on the amount you plan to give (or how you plan to give), you may want to speak to a CPA or financial planner.

| Funky | Trendy | Cool | Hip |

Wear The Music You Love!

Visit our merchandise store on our website:

WWW.FUNKTHERAPYMUSIC.COM

10% Discount code: STAYFUNKY

- Hoodies
- Crop Top
- Sweat Pants
- Bucket Hats
- Slides
- Mugs

UNISEX T-SHIRTS

Brown T-Shirt

GRAB IT NOW

Orange T-Shirt

GRAB IT NOW

Beige T-Shirts

GRAB IT NOW

Join our community
@funktherapy2